Private Life:
The house & tenement house.
Height of tenement houses limited
by Augustus to 70 ft & by
Nero to 60 ft

THE ARCHITECTURE
OF ANCIENT ROME

5-9

THE ARCHITECTURE
OF ANCIENT ROME

AN ACCOUNT OF ITS HISTORIC
DEVELOPMENT

BEING THE SECOND PART OF

THE ARCHITECTURE
OF GREECE AND ROME

BY

WILLIAM J. ANDERSON, A.R.I.B.A.
Author of " The Architecture of the Renaissance in Italy "

AND

R. PHENÉ SPIERS, F.S.A., F.R.I.B.A.
Author of " Architecture East and West "

REVISED AND REWRITTEN BY

THOMAS ASHBY, D.Litt., F.S.A.
Late Director of the British School at Rome

LONDON
B. T. BATSFORD LTD., 94 HIGH HOLBORN

PREFACE TO THE NEW EDITION.

THE history of Roman architecture is perhaps more difficult to write at the present time than at any other. The critical examination of materials and methods of construction and of architectural forms has entered upon quite a new stage and a number of new problems present themselves for solution. We now see the urgent need of an investigation of the oldest buildings in Rome in order to determine the various quarries from which the Romans derived their materials, and the approximate dates at which they came into use[1]. Delbrück in his *Hellenistische Bauten in Latium*, in which he attempts, courageously but not altogether successfully, owing to certain defects with which we shall deal in the text, to prove that the Roman architecture of the last two centuries of the Republic owes everything to the Hellenism of the Eastern Mediterranean, while he cites an enormous number of examples from other lands, acknowledges at every turn that the material available for comparison is insufficient, and that he has often had to generalize on inadequate data.

Miss E. B. Van Deman's investigations into the dating of Roman concrete monuments[2] are equally valuable for the chronology of the Imperial period. To take a single example, it is to her that we owe the certainty that the whole of the superstructure of the Temple of Venus in Rome is, as it stands, the work of Maxentius, and contemporary with the adjacent Basilica Nova which he erected, but which, since his death has borne the name of Constantine.

On the other hand we have the late Comm. Rivoira maintaining successfully in his *Lombardic Architecture* and *Roman Architecture*, that Imperial Rome gave to Byzantium and the East[3] more than she took, and that the great question of " Orient oder Rom " could not be answered as German scholars had answered it, by making Rome dependent on Byzantium.

---

[1] Tenney, Frank, *Roman Buildings of the Republic.*
[2] *A.J.A.* XVI (1912), 230, 387.
[3] As far as Persia as Delbrück points out (*Op. cit.* II. 94).

MADE AND PRINTED IN GREAT BRITAIN
By McCorquodale & Co., Ltd., London
1927

The enlargement of our sphere of knowledge, the introduction of more accurate habits of observation (and of more adequate processes of reproduction), and the growth of a more critical spirit are factors which, while they may lead to a temporary unsettling of what was hitherto generally accepted[1] must inevitably lead (and have indeed already led) to the strengthening of the basis of our knowledge, so that upon it we may build up a structure which no longer rests upon the sand, but has a more sure and permanent foundation. It is with this object in view that the enlarged British School at Rome offers facilities to students of Architecture to come and study the original monuments on the spot and not merely from drawings and photographs, which however great their excellence, can never give a really adequate idea of the original, still less of its surroundings.

A word in conclusion as to the present revision. I have done my best, while retaining the many valuable features of the late Professor Spiers' work, to bring it into accordance with the progress of research and study in the interval. In the process, more and more changes have been introduced; and while some passages have been retained unaltered, others are perhaps hardly recognisable.

Such a task is never an easy one; and I hope that the archæologist has not imposed too much of his own methods and personality upon his readers, the majority of whom will undoubtedly be members, present or future, of the architectural profession.

ROME.   THOMAS ASHBY.
    March, 1927.

---

[1]As one example out of many I may take the deletion of the passages which in the previous edition (pp. 166, 252) dealt with the *Tepidarium* of the Baths of Agrippa. It is clear from Hülsen's careful study (*Die Thermen des Agrippa* (Rome, 1910), cf. esp. p. 13) that though "the name of its originator has long lent a high authority to this (Palladio's) plan, Uggeri, Canina and their numerous followers have either simply taken it over, or used it with slight corrections as the basis of their representations; and yet it would be easy to demonstrate, that in the main it is a creation of phantasy, on the analogy of the Baths of Caracalla, in which the existing remains are disregarded."

The insecurity of the whole subject of dating at present is shown by Delbrück's readiness (*Hell-Bauten* II. 43) to throw over the second century B.C., dating he had proposed for the two Ionic Temples in the Forum Holitorium (*Drei Tempel* 24, 50) in favour of the first century dating given by Wissowa (*Gött. Gel. Anz.* 1903, 563, cf. Fiechter *Röm. Mitt.* 1906—278) though much of his constructive work naturally goes by the board therewith. Cf. Frank, *op.cit.*

There is a similar uncertainty and inconsistency about his dating of the Temple at Segni.

Despite Stryzgowski's continued attempts to prove his thesis, I cannot, I confess, accept it,[1] and for me Rivoira's opinions, though exaggerated perhaps in some points of detail, are right in the main. We need far more first-hand work like his—he had at least seen the greater part of the monuments he mentions—and this is the more important, for the old publications are no longer adequate for modern requirements. The Princeton Expedition to Syria has set before itself the revisiting of all the sites and monuments that De Vogüé had seen. Is it too much to hope that Roman architecture may at length be entirely emancipated from Canina, who has to be quoted, *faute de mieux*, in so many cases ? This could easily be done were the best work of the students of the French Academy in Rome, now supplemented by the American Academy and the British School at Rome, to be taken as a basis. Much of the former has already been published in the *Monuments Antiques*, though on none too large a scale ; and the scope of this work could be extended so as to form a collection which would include all the important monuments of Rome and Italy, and to include the work of architects of other nationalities.

In the course of such a work the architect, in co-operation with the archæologist, would be able to solve many problems which at present block the way to a proper understanding of Roman architecture and its development.

We need, as the late Comm. Boni remarked years ago, " a grammar of mouldings " ; and a really careful study of the details of each building, proceeding from the known to the unknown, from accurately dated to undated monuments would probably bring us to something approaching certainty far sooner than one might at first sight be inclined to think. The late Fritz Toebelmann began such a work in regard to entablatures, and it is now being continued by Hülsen and Fiechter. Some students of architecture may be inclined to regard the archæologist as a tiresome sceptic ; but it is not only in architecture, but in history, in philosophy and in most other branches of knowledge as well, that the statements which have hitherto been confidently made by one writer after another are being found to require accurate testing by a re-examination of the actual material with which they have to deal.

---

[1] The actual examples he is able to quote in his *Origins of Christian Church Art* (Oxford, 1923, tr. by Dalton and Braunholtz) are too late in date to provide sufficient proof in face of the multitudinous examples of earlier date in the West.

Despite Stryzgowski's continued attempts to prove his thesis, I cannot, I confess, accept it,[1] and for me Rivoira's opinions, though exaggerated perhaps in some points of detail, are right in the main. We need far more first-hand work like his—he had at least seen the greater part of the monuments he mentions—and this is the more important, for the old publications are no longer adequate for modern requirements. The Princeton Expedition to Syria has set before itself the revisiting of all the sites and monuments that De Vogüé had seen. Is it too much to hope that Roman architecture may at length be entirely emancipated from Canina, who has to be quoted, *faute de mieux*, in so many cases? This could easily be done were the best work of the students of the French Academy in Rome, now supplemented by the American Academy and the British School at Rome, to be taken as a basis. Much of the former has already been published in the *Monuments Antiques*, though on none too large a scale; and the scope of this work could be extended so as to form a collection which would include all the important monuments of Rome and Italy, and to include the work of architects of other nationalities.

In the course of such a work the architect, in co-operation with the archæologist, would be able to solve many problems which at present block the way to a proper understanding of Roman architecture and its development.

We need, as the late Comm. Boni remarked years ago, "a grammar of mouldings"; and a really careful study of the details of each building, proceeding from the known to the unknown, from accurately dated to undated monuments would probably bring us to something approaching certainty far sooner than one might at first sight be inclined to think. The late Fritz Toebelmann began such a work in regard to entablatures, and it is now being continued by Hülsen and Fiechter. Some students of architecture may be inclined to regard the archæologist as a tiresome sceptic; but it is not only in architecture, but in history, in philosophy and in most other branches of knowledge as well, that the statements which have hitherto been confidently made by one writer after another are being found to require accurate testing by a re-examination of the actual material with which they have to deal.

---

[1] The actual examples he is able to quote in his *Origins of Christian Church Art* (Oxford, 1923, tr. by Dalton and Braunholtz) are too late in date to provide sufficient proof in face of the multitudinous examples of earlier date in the West.

The enlargement of our sphere of knowledge, the introduction of more accurate habits of observation (and of more adequate processes of reproduction), and the growth of a more critical spirit are factors which, while they may lead to a temporary unsettling of what was hitherto generally accepted[1] must inevitably lead (and have indeed already led) to the strengthening of the basis of our knowledge, so that upon it we may build up a structure which no longer rests upon the sand, but has a more sure and permanent foundation. It is with this object in view that the enlarged British School at Rome offers facilities to students of Architecture to come and study the original monuments on the spot and not merely from drawings and photographs, which however great their excellence, can never give a really adequate idea of the original, still less of its surroundings.

A word in conclusion as to the present revision. I have done my best, while retaining the many valuable features of the late Professor Spiers' work, to bring it into accordance with the progress of research and study in the interval. In the process, more and more changes have been introduced ; and while some passages have been retained unaltered, others are perhaps hardly recognisable.

Such a task is never an easy one ; and I hope that the archæologist has not imposed too much of his own methods and personality upon his readers, the majority of whom will undoubtedly be members, present or future, of the architectural profession.

Rome.   Thomas Ashby.
March, 1927.

---

[1]As one example out of many I may take the deletion of the passages which in the previous edition (pp. 166, 252) dealt with the *Tepidarium* of the Baths of Agrippa. It is clear from Hülsen's careful study (*Die Thermen des Agrippa* (Rome, 1910), cf. esp. p. 13) that though " the name of its originator has long lent a high authority to this (Palladio's) plan, Uggeri, Canina and their numerous followers have either simply taken it over, or used it with slight corrections as the basis of their representations ; and yet it would be easy to demonstrate, that in the main it is a creation of phantasy, on the analogy of the Baths of Caracalla, in which the existing remains are disregarded."

The insecurity of the whole subject of dating at present is shown by Delbrück's readiness (*Hell-Bauten* II. 43) to throw over the second century B.C., dating he had proposed for the two Ionic Temples in the Forum Holitorium (*Drei Tempel* 24, 50) in favour of the first century dating given by Wissowa (*Gött. Gel. Anz.* 1903, 563, cf. Fiechter *Röm. Mitt.* 1906—278) though much of his constructive work naturally goes by the board therewith. Cf. Frank, *op.cit.*

There is a similar uncertainty and inconsistency about his dating of the Temple at Segni.

PREFACE TO FIRST EDITION.

To the late William J. Anderson, of Glasgow, is due the conception of this work. The course of lectures which, on the invitation of the Governors of the School of Art in that city, he delivered in 1893–94 on the Architecture of the Renaissance in Italy (published in 1896), was followed in 1896–97 by a course on the History and Development of Greek Architecture. To this subject he devoted his studies for three years, repeating his course with various revisions, and adding to it in 1897 three additional lectures on Roman Architecture, which, with those on Greek, he intended to publish as his second work. Immediately following these Roman lectures, he continued, in 1898, with a course which included the various styles down to the present day, and in the winter of 1898–99 a further special course dealing with the Renaissance in France.

The preparation of these courses would seem to have interfered with the studies he intended to devote to Roman Architecture in order to bring them in line with the Greek. There is no doubt that he had attained a masterly grasp of the principles underlying Greek work, more particularly those dealing with the Archaic and culminating periods, the study of which would seem to have had a special attraction for him. It was his intention to deal with Roman work in the same way, and with that in view, and being in indifferent health, he expressed the desire that I, who had been in frequent communication with him respecting the various courses he had delivered, should undertake to read and see through the press the chapters on Greek Architecture (for which, as well as for the Roman, numerous illustrations had already been prepared), so as to give him more time to devote to those on Roman Architecture. He died, however, before this intention was realised, and the whole work was then placed in my hands by Mr. Batsford with the entire concurrence of Mr. Anderson's widow.

In parts of the work there are some theories put forward which have not yet obtained universal acceptance; but one of the

objects has been to stimulate the student's interest in the subject, with the hope that, by independent research, he may ascertain for himself, either among the treasures of the British and other museums, or in the numerous publications cited in the Bibliography, how far those theories can be substantiated.

R. PHENÉ SPIERS.

LONDON,
  September, 1902.

NOTE OF ACKNOWLEDGMENT.

I have to thank Mr. H. Chalton Bradshaw for kindly permitting the reproduction of a number of his valuable reconstructions, including his plan of the central portion of Ancient Rome and his drawing of Præneste : also for his valuable assistance in reading through the proofs of this volume during my own absence in America. I must also make acknowledgment of the original sources of a number of the illustrations. The subjects on Plates VIII, XIV$_{(3)}$ and XX originally appeared in the Papers of the British School at Rome, and are reproduced by permission ; those on Plates XXXVII and XLV appear by permission of the Royal Institute of British Architects, from the Journal of the Institute ; the photograph of the early wall on the Quirinal Hill on Plate IV, and the subjects on Plates XII, LXII$_{(2)}$ and LXVI by permission of the Italian Ministry of Public Instruction ; and those on Plates LXVII and LXIX by permission of the Journal of Roman Studies, in which they appeared. I am also grateful for the use of a number of original drawings, reconstructions, &c., the names of whose authors appear beneath the reproductions.

Of the remaining subjects, those on Plates II$_{(2)}$ and III$_{(2)}$ are reproduced from original photographs by Mr. R. Gardner; that on Plate LXVII$_{(1)}$ by Mr. R. A. L. Fell; on Plate X$_{(3)}$ by Mr. P. K. Baillie-Reynolds ; on Plate LIX$_{(1)}$ by Monsieur L. Poinssot, Director of Antiquities at Tunis. Those on Plates V$_{(3)}$, LV$_{(2)}$, LXII$_{(1)}$ and LXVIII$_{(2)}$ are from photographs by the Rev. Father P. P. Mackey, O.P. ; on Plates XLIII$_{(2)}$ and LXVIII$_{(1)}$ by Miss D. E. Bulwer ; on Plates II$_{(1)}$, V$_{(2)}$, VI$_{(1, 2)}$, IX$_{(1, 2)}$, XV, XLIV, and XCI$_{(2)}$ by Messrs. Alinari, to all of whom I must tender my grateful thanks for their inclusion.

T. A.

CHRONOLOGICAL MEMORANDA.

6th cent. B.C. Cloaca Maxima built.

509 B.C. Republic established.

309 „ Subjugation of S. Etruria.

323 „ Hellenistic period from the death of Alexander the Great.

270 „ Supremacy of Rome in Italy.

241 „ Sicily annexed by Rome. *1st Punic war 264 - 241*

146 „ Destruction of Carthage and Corinth.

86 „ Sulla captures the Piræus and Athens.

78 „ Tabularium built by Catulus.

49 „ Julius Cæsar proclaimed dictator.

44 „ Assassination of Julius Cæsar.

31 „ Victory of Augustus at Actium.

ROMAN EMPIRE.*

27 B.C.–14 A.D. Augustus.

14–37 A.D. Tiberius.

37–41 „ Caligula.

41–54 „ Claudius.

54–68 „ Nero.

69–79 „ Vespasian.

79–81 „ Titus.

81–96 „ Domitian.

96–98 „ Nerva.

98–117 „ Trajan.

117–138 A.D. Hadrian.

138–161 „ Antoninus Pius.

161–180 „ Marcus Aurelius.

180–192 „ Commodus.

193–211 „ Septimius Severus.

212–217 „ Caracalla.

284–305 „ Diocletian.

306–337 „ Constantine.

* Only the more important Emperors are given.

CONTENTS.

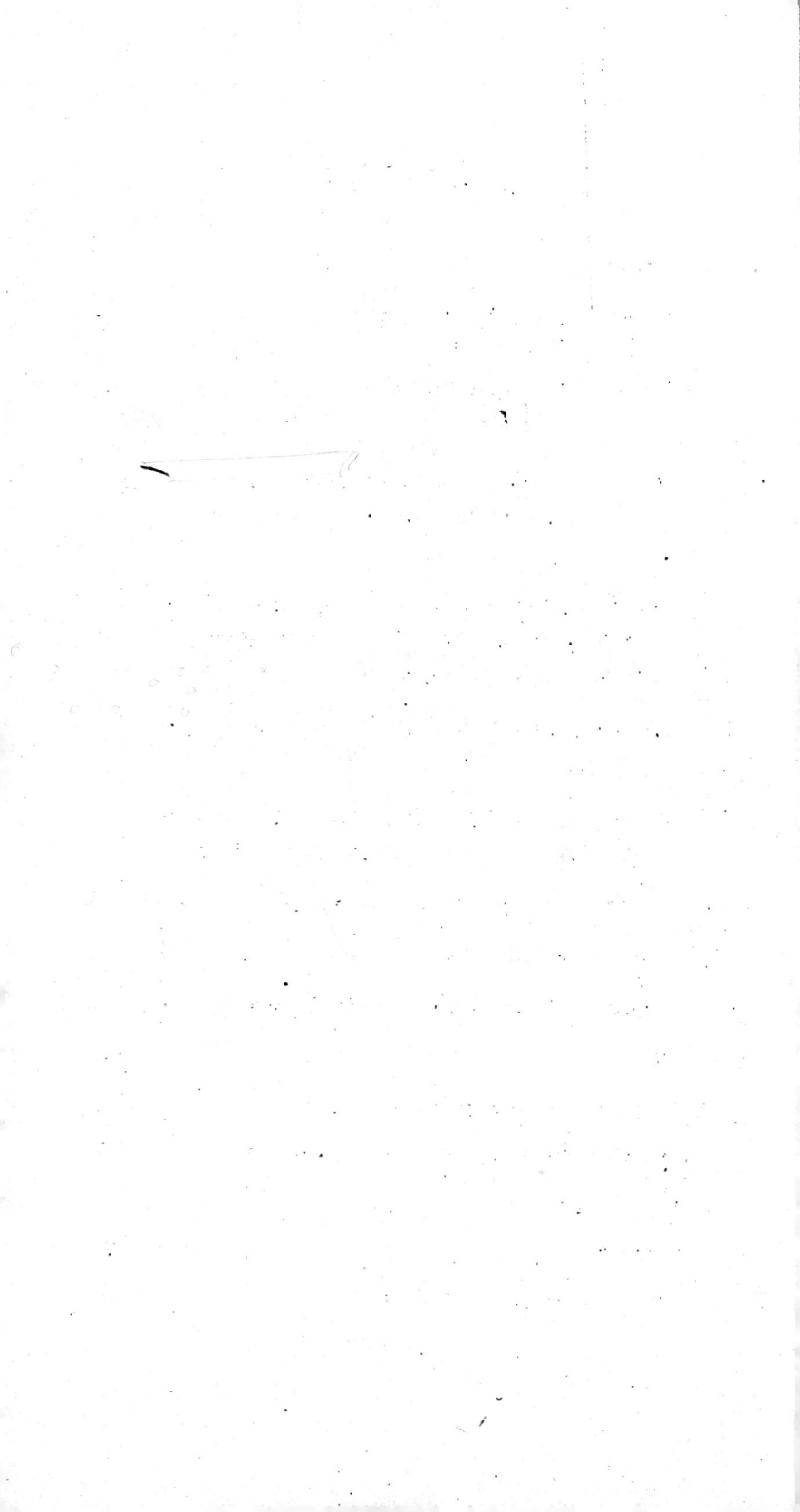

CHAPTER I

ARCHITECTURE IN ETRURIA AND ELSEWHERE IN ITALY DOWN TO THE END OF THE THIRD CENTURY B.C.

THE problems connected with the movements of population in the Italian peninsula before the beginning of the historical period are too complicated and difficult to be discussed here, and have, in any case, little bearing on architecture. The most primitive form of architecture, if it may be called so, is the hut. The round hut common to all nomadic peoples, which makes its appearance in Italy in the neolithic, or later stone, age, is important as the embryo of the circular temple.[1] Similarly the circular burial mound developed into such great mausolea as the tomb of Caecilia Metella and the mausolea of Augustus and Hadrian. The hut urns of the early iron age are, on the other hand, almost rectangular in plan, though the sides and ends are curved.

Again, we find that the early bronze civilization of the inhabitants of the *terremare*, as they are called, had advanced so far that they had developed for themselves the trapezoidal ground plan (Fig. 1), and some archæologists account for the choice of the Palatine as the nucleus of Rome by the fact that settlers from the *terremare* recognized its suitability to their purposes.[2]

---

[1] The Greek temples of S. Italy and Sicily are be dealt with in the companion volume to this work, *viz.*, *The Architecture of Greece* (W. J. Anderson and R. Ph. Spiers), revised by W. B. Dinsmoor (Batsford, 1926).

[2] The scepticism of Sergi, who believes that all so-called *terremare* which present a rectangular plan are in reality Roman camps, will not hold against the facts. *L'Italia, le origini* pp. 245-91 : contrast Pigorini in *Archivio Storico per la Sicilia Orientale* xvi (pp. 7, 8 of reprint), who maintains that the choice of the Palatine by the earliest settlers was due to its trapezoidal shape. It is really, however, far more probable that it is to be attributed to the fact that this hill commanded the only crossing of the Tiber in the whole of its lower course—a crossing which was probably in use long before any settlement existed on the site.

A

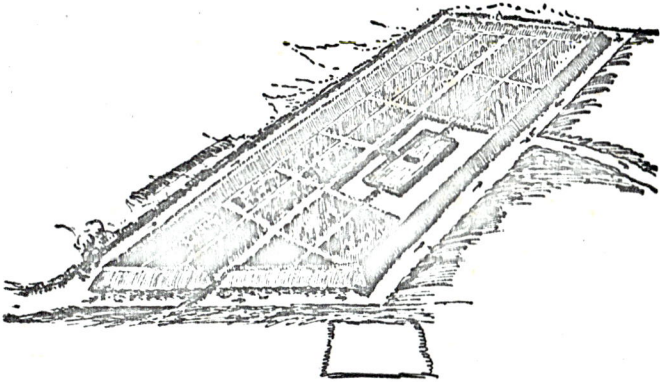

FIG. 1.—PLAN OF A TERREMARE.

The traditional date of the foundation of Rome (753 B.C.) which, as recent discoveries have shown, may be regarded as approximately correct, falls in the same century as the coming of the earliest Greek settlers to Southern Italy and Sicily.   But the origin and affinities of the Etruscans, and the date of their arrival in the portion of Central Italy which bears their name (though they were by no means exclusively confined to it) are as yet unknown ; though it is quite certain that in the latter part of the Regal period Rome was under Etruscan domination.   The earliest monuments of architecture which can be associated with them are an important class of tombs, belonging apparently to their chieftains, the majority of which date from *ca.* 650-600 B.C.   They generally consisted of a huge mound of earth, with a low retaining wall round its outer circumference, in which one or more chambers formed the actual burial place.   The roof, whether domed (as at Mycenae[1]) or not,[2] is formed by the projection one over another of horizontal courses of stone.   In the entrance wall of the Campana tomb at Veii, though the same system is adopted, there is a keystone at the top, and also in some of the tombs at Orvieto (sixth-fourth centuries B.C.).   There are subterranean structures in Rome itself of approximately the same date with corbelled vaults in which the principle of the arch is either unknown or ignored[3]—the lower chamber of the so-called

---

[1] Cf. A. Garroni: *Studi d'Antichita*, 93 *sqq.*

[2] Notable examples of the former will be found at Volterra and Vetulonia, of the latter at Caere in the "tomba Regolini-Galassi" and in other tombs.

[3] I should not be prepared to affirm that in subterranean constructions this may not have been adopted as a more convenient way of covering a space than a segmental dome.

B

THE PORTA SANGUINARIA, FERENTINO.

POINTED ARCH IN THE REGOLINI GALASSI
TOMB, CERVETERI.

PLATE III.

EARLY CISTERN ON THE
PALATINE.

EARLY DRAIN NEAR THE
TEMPLE OF SATURN.

PORTA SARACINESCA, SIGNIA.

Mamertine Prison, or Tullianum, and some early cisterns on the Palatine, only one of which is at present visible to the public (Plate III)[1]. The arch itself, both round and pointed, dates from time immemorial ; and Professor Petrie's discovery at Dendera, in Egypt, of passages 6 feet wide, covered with barrel vaults of three rings of voussoirs built in crude brick, and dating from 3,500 B.C., shows that, as a method of construction, the arched vault must have been one of the earliest known methods of covering over space. The actual employment, however, of regular voussoirs in stone, cannot, it would seem, be traced in any monument earlier than the temple tombs of the High-priestesses of Thebes at Medinet-Abu (700-650 B.C.)[2] ; and, as far as we can at present judge, the next stone vaults in point of date are some early drains built of " cappellaccio " (a soft dark gray tufa—green when wet—which splits easily into horizontal layers) at the north-west end of the Forum in Rome (Plate III), which can be attributed to the end of the sixth or the beginning of the fifth century B.C.[3], for considerable remains of other buildings of this period also exist, built of the same material, which is cut into slabs rather than blocks, about a foot high, two or three long and two or three deep. This material and form of construction (which is peculiar to the city of Rome, and due to this special material) is to be found in the podiums of the temples of Jupiter Capitolinus (recently brought to light), Saturn, and Castor and Pollux, and in other minor monuments,[4] and there are scanty remains of a defensive wall built in this style on the Palatine[5] (Fig. 2) while the same technique may be seen in the remains of the first stone wall by which the city of Rome was fortified (Plate IV),

---

[1] The date of the cistern at Tusculum (*Papers of the British School at Rome*, V. p. 357 and Pl. XXX, Fig. 2) must be regarded as uncertain.

[2] Delbrück : *Hellenistische Bauten in Latium*. II, 80 sqq.

[3] I cannot agree with Tenney Frank, *Roman Buildings of the Republic*, 52 sqq. that these drains served to carry away the blood of victims slain at altars. He assigns them to the fourth century.

[4] We may instance the earliest form of the Cloaca Maxima, of the shrine of Venus Cloacina, and of the Lacus Curtius. The Temple of Apollo is slightly later (431 B.C.). Tenney Frank's arguments (*op. cit.* 131 sqq.) do not, it seems to me, prove that the core is not part of the original structure. We get in it, as in the earlier city wall, traces of Greek influence in "anathyrosis," the beds and joints being worked away so that the blocks touch only along the edge.

[5] " Its preservation is due to the fact that at a later time a second circuit wall was built in the technique of the ' Servian ' walls of Rome, about 2½ feet in front of the old fortification, while both of these were afterwards encased by the concrete substructures of Imperial buildings." (Stuart Jones : *Companion to Roman History*, 31, Fig. 7, from which our illustration, Fig. 2, is taken).

which is probably to be attributed to the same period.[1] The claim hitherto advanced on behalf of the Etruscans, that it was from them that the Romans learnt the construction of the arch (if indeed they learnt it from anyone, and it is not rather an independent development) can only be sustained in the sense that the last Kings

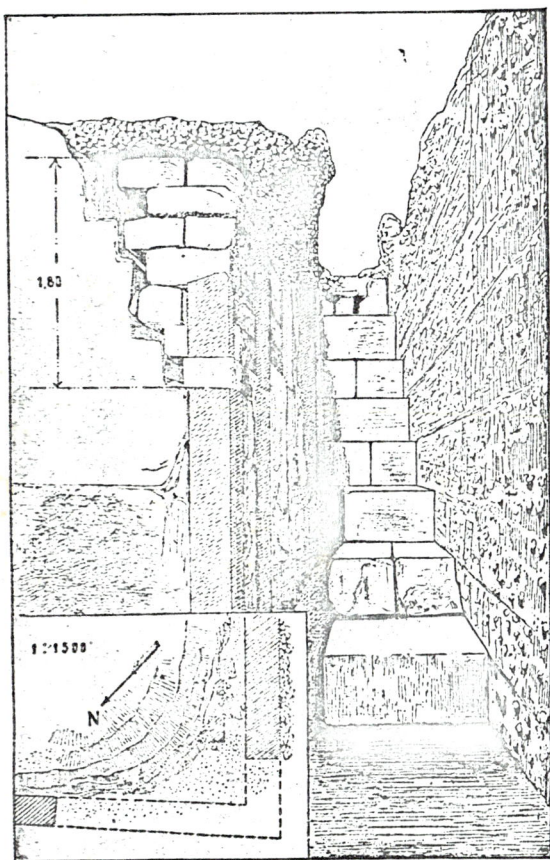

Fig. 2.—Early Fortification Walls on Palatine.

[1] *American Journal of Archæology* (1918): 175 *sqq.* and *op. cit.* 90 *sqq.* He there re-states an earlier view that the Aventine was not enclosed within the original Servian wall, and attributes the wall on the Palatine (there is more doubt about the gateway found—and destroyed—near S. Maria in Cosmedin in 1886) to this original seventh and sixth century, B.C. fortification. Delbrück (*Apollotempel*, pp. 13-15) wishes to assign the Palatine wall to the sixth century and the rest of the enceinte to 379 B.C., after the fire of the Gauls despite their similarity of style.

of Rome, the Tarquins, to whom the erection of the Temple of Jupiter and the Cloaca Maxima (Plate IV) is ascribed, were of Etruscan lineage. ✕ For there are no true arches[1] to be found in Etruria itself until we get to the fourth and third centuries B.C.—to which epoch the city gates of Perugia[2] (Fig. 3, Plate V), Volterra, Falerii (Plate IV), must be attributed—while the masonry of the sixth century B.C. in Etruria, as instanced by the walls of Volterra and Cortona, has nothing of the technical perfection which is to be found in even the earlier walls of Rome. South of Rome, too, in the Volscian and Hernican mountains, we meet with numerous hill towns, which still preserve imposing remains of their " Cyclopean " walls of huge many-sided blocks of the native limestone, some of them having gates in which the principle of the arch is not employed. The Porta Saracinesca at Segni (Plate III) is perhaps the best known example ; but we may also mention the Porta dell' Arco at Arpino, in which the principle of the inclination of the sides is employed to an even greater extent, though a flat lintel was used in both cases. At Alatri, on the other hand, both in the Porta di Civita and in another minor gate there is little or no inclination of the sides. In others, e.g. at Ferentino, the upper part is in ashlar masonry of softer limestone, contemporary with the rest of the wall (Plate II).

The belief, once universally held, in the high antiquity of these constructions has long ago been given up. Recent investigations at Norba, indeed, have shown that these walls do not go further back than about 500 B.C., and the contrast between the exterior and the interior of the walls of Circeii will be instructive to those who have hitherto held that greater refinement of construction necessarily connotes a difference in date. Choisy's interpretation

---

[1] The " canal on the Marta at Graviscae " on which many writers have relied as evidence for the development of the arch in Etruria at a very early period is in reality a bridge of the Via Aurelia, the Roman coast road of about 180 B.C. : while recent investigations have shown that the Cloaca Maxima, unlike its branch drains, was originally an open drain (Hulsen : *Roman Forum* p. 5), and was only roofed, at the earliest, about 184 B.C. Our illustration shows its mouth, where it is about 11 feet wide with 3 concentric rings of voussoirs, each about 2 feet 6 inches in height.

[2] It must be borne in mind that the date of this arch is much discussed, some authorities maintaining that the upper part is Roman, though the form of the capitals is against them. The question is closely connected with that of the date of the Porta Marzia (Pl. V), a city gate which was destroyed in the sixteenth century of which the upper part only is preserved. The inscription on this was probably added by Augustus.

FIG. 3.—THE ARCH OF AUGUSTUS AT PERUGIA.

PLATE IV.

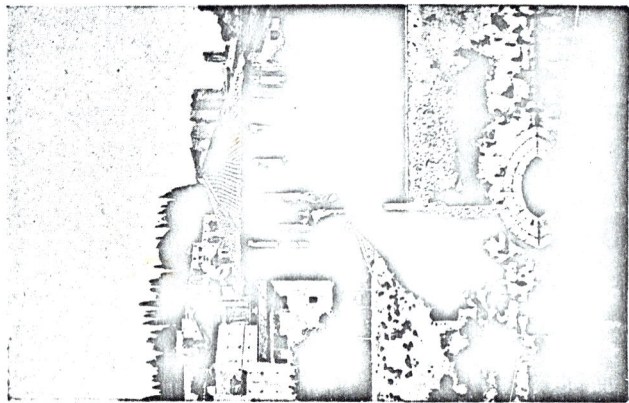

THE CLOACA MAXIMA.

EARLY WALL OF ROME ON THE QUIRINAL HILL.

PORTA DEL BOVE, FALERII.

EMBANKMENT OF VIA APPIA AT ITRI.

PORTA MARZIA, PERUGIA.

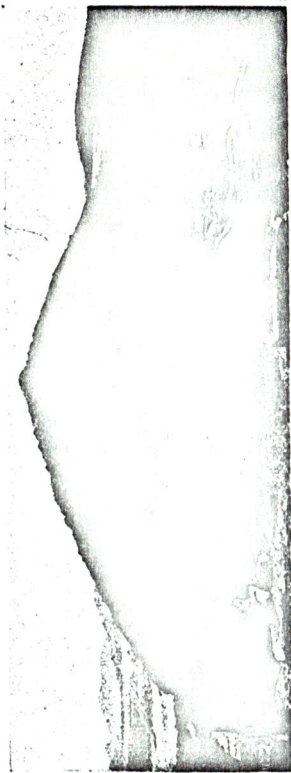

CIRCULAR TOMB AT CERVETERI.

of the differences of construction to which we have alluded is undoubtedly the right one—" in districts where the stone does not
split in the grain, polygonal construction is a necessity ; coursed
masonry is indicated wherever the quarry presents horizontal
stratification. We are dealing with a geological fact far more
than with a question of date." [1]   Thus we find embankment walls
on Roman high roads of the fourth and third centuries B.C. in limestone country, as for example on the Via Appia (Plate V) and the
Via Salaria,[2] still constructed in the older style, the culverts not
being arched, but having converging sides and flat lintels[3] ; and
the " polygonal " style of masonry was employed owing to its
decorative value for the terrace walls of Roman villas at the end
of the Republic, and the beginning of the Empire, and is used even
nowadays for revetting earth embankments, where it is not worth
while to hew the hard stone into rectangular blocks.

After the capture of Rome by the Gauls in 391 B.C. the city wall
was rebuilt, and to this period belongs the enceinte generally known
as the " Servian " wall, in which the standard block, 4 Roman feet
in length and 2 feet square at the end, is employed, so that the alter-
nation of headers and stretchers is easy and indeed natural. The
original wall of cappellaccio was in some places used as the retaining
wall for the agger or earth embankment which was added at all
weak points.

Turning now to Etruscan tombs we find that they fall into two
main classes : (1) immense *tumuli* or mounds of earth, the bases of
which are surrounded by a stone wall (Plate V). Within these
mounds are burial chambers. Sometimes, as at Cervetri, the base
with its moulding, and the sepulchral chambers within, are hewn
out of the solid rock ; (2) Smaller rectangular chamber tombs,
without *tumuli* above them, but presenting similar characteristics
internally. An insight into the domestic architecture of the
Etruscans is best obtained from the second class of tombs, though
the recent discovery in Sardinia of two tombs, in one of which we
have the actual imitation of the poles supporting the thatched roof
of a circular hut, while in the other we have a close parallel to the
false timber roofs of the Etruscan tombs, which are certainly a good

---

[1] *Histoire de l'Architecture*, I, 229.

[2] See *Papers of the British School at Rome*, III.   Pl. II.   Figs. 3, 4.

[3] I have noticed a similar method of roofing in the platform of a Roman
villa at Scauri on the coast between Gaeta and Naples.

deal later in date, may indicate that the prototype was actually Sardinian, or at any rate not exclusively Etruscan.[1]

The principal chamber in one of the tombs at Corneto probably represents the atrium of an Etruscan house, which corresponds to the description given in Vitruvius (vi. 3) of the simpler type of the Roman atrium, viz., the " cavaedium displuviatum " in which there was an opening at the top, the roof sloping down towards the sides. The rafters which carried the roof are copied on the ceiling, which slopes down on each side. Similar reproductions of the timbers of the roof are shown in other tombs at Cervetri and elsewhere : in one instance, a flat roof or ceiling with joists ; in a second, a roof with a central ridge across the room, the rafters sloping down on each side (Plate VI). In another well-known tomb (also at Cervetri) additional support to the roof is given by square piers with volute capitals (Plate VI). In this tomb are recesses in the wall which suggest the chambers round the atrium, and are here utilised as cubicles for the dead bodies ; whilst the walls and piers are carved with representations of the household utensils, weapons, etc., as they might have been hanging in the house.

The exterior of such a house is represented upon an urn from Chiusi, now in Berlin (*Beschr. d. Skulpt.* no. 1242 : Durm ii, fig. 43). The type corresponds with that of the oldest Pompeian house (*ib.* fig. 41 ; Mau-Kelsey, *Pompeii*, p. 246). The well-known hut urn, on the other hand represents the rectangular type of the simple shepherd's hut with a single room. The doorways of rock cut tombs too were often copied from domestic architecture, and two or three are often joined together by a series of mouldings above them. Two more elaborate examples, one from Sovana, the other from Norchia, are here shown (Plate VII)[2] in the latter the pediments ; and columns of temple facades are imitated.

The most important decorations in the Etruscan tombs are the friezes, with figures in procession, dancing, feasting, etc., painted in bright colours.

In regard to Etruscan temples, our knowledge has progressed very considerably. Prof. A. Della Seta (*Museo di Villa Giulia* I, p. 121-166 (Rome, Danesi, 1918)) in his masterly treatment of the whole subject of Etruscan terracottas, has the following passage:

---

[1] Taramelli in *Mon. Lincei*, XXV, 861 *sqq.*

[2] From drawings by S. J. Ainsley in the Department of Prints and Drawings in the British Museum.

"Just as the oldest Greek temples do not correspond,[1] in many elements of plan, structure and decoration, with the fixed type which the theorists of later days gave as proper to the Doric and Ionic order, but only mark, through the gradual elimination of individual elements, that progress towards the rigid canon which proclaims the decadence of art and the triumph of academic teaching, so excavations have made it clear that the type of Tuscan temple described by Vitruvius, instead of being the original one, is comparatively late and has been made still more rigid by his didactic exposition of it. . . . . . Vitruvius' temple is distinguished in plan from the Greek temple by its greater breadth in proportion to its length ; and this is a necessary consequence of the triplication of the cella, inasmuch as three divinities were contained in three separate compartments. The length of the pronaos was equal to that of the cellae : two columns on each side were placed on the line of the external walls, equidistant from one another, and two others were placed on the line of the walls of the central cella between them and the front line of columns (see plan and elevation, Plate VIII, of a temple at Falerii Veteres, the modern Civita Castellana). He does not say anything of a *posticum*. As to the elevation, beyond the proportions of the columns and the capital, the only certain datum that can be obtained from Vitruvius' description is the fact that the roof projected considerably beyond the walls of the cella, though there is some disagreement as to the amount of this projection . . . . . In order to make up for the scantiness of the data furnished by Vitruvius, careful study has been devoted to monuments which reproduced the temple on a small scale (cippi, cinerary urns, sarcophagi, votive shrines) ; but recourse has been had in still greater measure to excavations, which have been conducted in the whole territory occupied by the Etruscans from the Po southwards, and, outside Etruria, in Latium and Umbria. If these excavations have thrown little light on the superstructure of the Etruscan temple (for its walls and trabeation have for the most part perished irremediably) they have, on the other hand, made it clear that its plan, especially in the earliest times, differs from the Vitruvian type, the length being more important than the breadth, so that it can be more or less referred to the Greek type with its lengthened cella and pronaos, the proportions

---

[1] See also Mrs. S. Arthur Strong in *Journal of Roman Studies*, IV (1914), 157; and Taylor and Bradshaw in *Papers of the British School at Rome*, VIII (1916) 1 *sqq.* (from Pl. I of which our Plate VIII is taken).

C

of which may vary, but not more, relatively, than those of the treasuries or sacred shrines of Olympia and Delphi. Whether this type of building was imported from Greece, whence the inspiration of the terracotta decoration was certainly derived, or whether it is the imitation of an Italic building, the house, is a problem which as yet remains unsolved . . . .

As regard the relations between this elongated type of temple, which appears to be the oldest, and the broader plan described by Vitruvius, the existence of which has also been proved by excavation, but only in a later period, we may fairly suppose that the plan and proportions of the latter owe their peculiarities to the exigencies of worship . . . . As regards the superstructure of the Italic temple . . . . it is clear from the excavations that the use of stone in the construction was restricted to the foundations of the walls of the cella and of the columns . . . the walls as a rule up to the trabeation being of brick. It is only in the fourth century B.C. that we find temples with stone cellae, and monolithic columns appear in the same period, while before this time the column was built up of masonry or made of wood and sometimes cased with slabs of terracotta. The trabeation was always of wood even when the cella walls were of stone. It consists of the framework of the gable roof, which rested laterally on the walls of the cella, and formed a triangular pediment in front and behind. The most important elements of this framework were the tiebeam (*columen*) which formed as it were the backbone of the roof, the lateral beams (*mutuli*) which rested on the cella walls, the " cavalle " (*cantherii*) which rested on the *columen* and on the *mutuli*, the smaller beams (*templa*) parallel to the *columen* and the *mutuli* which rested on the *cantherii*. The framework was concealed laterally by the terracotta decoration and above by the tile roof.

While excavations have given us but little information in regard to the plan and elevation of the Italic temple, the remains of their terracotta decoration have been discovered in such considerable quantity as to permit of our tracing the history of this branch of art with a reasonable approach to certainty. [See E. Douglas Van Buren. *Figurative Terracotta Revetments in Etruria and Latium and Archaic Fictile Revetments in Sicily and Magna Græcia.*] One fact deserves to be emphasised at once, inasmuch as it is in agreement with what had been proved by numerous other archæological

D

PLATE VI.

TOMBA DELL ALCOVA, CERVETERI.

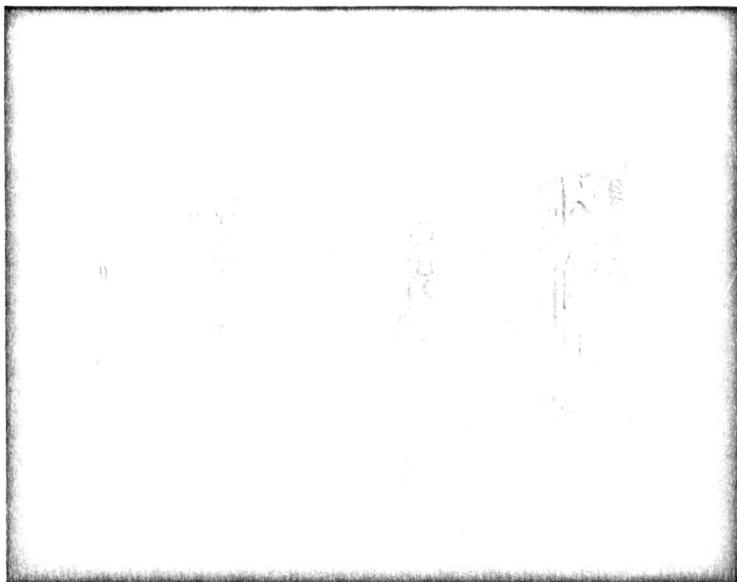

TOMBA DEGLI STUCCHI, CERVETERI.

PLATE VII.

ROCK-CUT TOMB AT SOVANA.

ROCK-CUT TOMB AT NORCHIA.

Both from the drawings by S. J. Ainsley, in Department of Prints and Drawings, British Museum.

finds, and helps to determine the position of Etruscan art in the general scheme of the art of Italy. In the same way as the industrial products of the so-called Oriental period of the seventh century B.C. appear both in Etruria and in Latium and Campania and in the same way as these territories present other products of Greek art in the sixth, fifth and fourth centuries B.C., a fact which proves that the same artists worked both for the Etruscans and their neighbours, so the decoration of the Etruscan temple (which for this very reason should rather be called Italic) appears with the same technique, the same forms and the same subjects beyond the boundaries of Etruria, in Umbria, Latium and Campania.[1] [One of the main differences between the terracotta decoration of Etruscan and the Greek temples is the presence in the latter of lateral external friezes which take the place of the metopes and triglyphs.]

That the terracottas are of local manufacture is proved both by the clay of which they are made, by their nature (for it is only on the spot that they could have been made to fit the building for which they were intended) by the letters and numbers painted or scratched on them, which are sometimes Greek, but more often of local origin, and still more by the discovery in some cases of the actual moulds. We must therefore suppose that they were the work of travelling artisans who carried some of the smaller moulds with them[2]; for it is not an art which bears the mark of a national civilization, but rather an imported art placed at the service of a variety of peoples and cults. Nor should its origin be sought in Etruria, where it was as much an importation as in Campania or Latium, but in Greece or in the nearer East. Terracotta temple decorations identical with those of the Italic temple have been found in Thessaly and in Asia Minor, while it is more difficult to find parallels to the terracottas of S. Italy and Sicily. But its guiding principle, its forms and subjects are all Greek; and it matters little whether it was the work of Greek artists or of Italians taught by Greeks.

A proof of this continued inspiration from Greece may be seen in the fact that this decoration never lost contact with the

---

[1] The numerous decorative terracottas, which have recently been brought to light in Syracuse belong to the seventh and sixth centuries B.C.: they are of the highest importance in the history of design, and it is clear from them that even if this method of decoration was Corinthian in origin, it was in Sicily that it attained its highest development (Orsi in *Mon. Lincei*, XXV, 354 ff.).

[2] This accounts for identity of type on different sites.

fountainhead ; but there was also a local tradition, the persistence of which is seen in the forms, motives, and conventions : thus, the conventional use of red to denote a man, and of white to denote a woman which goes back as far as the art of Greece and Mycenae, and was gradually given up by Greek art, is maintained as late as the third-second centuries B.C.

We may distinguish three periods in the decoration of the Italic temple—the first, belonging to the latter half of the sixth century B.C., in which we find cresting above the pediment and frieze slabs, antefixæ and acroteria ; the second to the end of the sixth and the first half of the fifth century (in which a more copious use of this decoration was made—frieze along the sides and bottom of the pediment, of the head of the *columen* and probably of the two *mutuli*, antefixæ along the bottom of the pediment, frieze along the sides : a new element, which perhaps belonged only to the sides, being pendant slabs fixed by leaden bolts to the edge of the gutter tiles (Plate IX) ; and the third, separated from the second by an interval of more than a century, which begins with the dawn of Hellenistic art at the end of the fourth century B.C., and goes as far as the second. In this period we find pedimental sculptures for the first time, the existence of which presupposes the abolition of the deep internal frame of the earlier form and of the decoration of the beam ends.[1] After this we find terracotta slabs used in the main only as the decoration of houses (the so-called Campana terracottas).

The example of a temple with three cellæ, shown in Plate VIII is a conjectural restoration. The temple of Jupiter Capitolinus, the most famous sacred building of ancient Rome, was certainly identical in plan, except for the addition of a peristyle on each side, making the front hexastyle. It stood, we know, on a podium[2] the remains of which have recently been brought to light by the demolition of the former German Embassy on the Capitol. It was founded by Tarquin I, and completed by his son in 509 B.C. It was decorated

---

[1] We may instance the terracottas from Conca as examples of the work of the seventh and fifth centuries, those of Segni of that of the fifth and third, and those of Alatri of that of the third. In no cases have the specimens preserved at the Museo di Villa Giulia been properly published, though all of them are well described in Della Seta's work.

[2] The podium is found in Etruria from the fifth century B.C. onwards, and it is from there that it came into Latium and S. Italy. Thus, the temple at Conca (seventh century B.C., rebuilt in the fifth) has no podium ; and the earliest podium temple appears in Central Italy (perhaps) in 302 B.C. (at Alba Fucens—see Delbrück : *Drei Tempel*, 26) ; in S. Italy in the third century B.C. the Corinthian Doric temple at Pæstum) ; and in Sicily even later.

with terracottas, of which only scanty remains have been found,[1] and the pediment was crowned by a quadriga in the same material. Pliny tells us that the decorations were the work of Vulca, a Veientine artist ; and striking light has been thrown on their character by the discovery at Veii itself of the temple of Apollo, with three cellæ, and considerable remains of terracotta decorations of this very period, as well as of important points of a group of life-size statues in the same material—by far the finest that have come down to us.[2]

This temple was burnt in the year 83 B.C., and reconstructed on the same plan by Sulla in the following year. This second temple was burnt in 70 A.D., rebuilt by Vespasian on the old plan, but with its height increased, and burnt again ten years later. The fourth temple was built by Domitian with greater splendour, and with Corinthian columns of Pentelic marble. A representation of the temple on a bas-relief from an Arch of Marcus Aurelius, now in the Palazzo dei Conservatori, shows the pediment filled with sculpture, with a reproduction of the famous terracotta quadriga (originally made at Veii for Tarquinius Superbus) on its summit, and a rich cresting rising above the pediment on each side.

Rome provides us with examples of other temples not very much later in date in which the podium is present (which in Greece it was not), but we cannot be certain of their dimensions. It seems unlikely, however, that the proportions of the earliest temple of Castor and Pollux (484 B.C.) differed much from that of the later (length to breadth 5 to 3)[3] and Della Seta's exposition seems to make it quite clear that the nearly square podia which are sometimes met with in Italy can only be explained by the fact that they were constructed for temples with three cellæ.[4]

As examples of the third period of Etruscan architecture we may take the rock cut tombs at Norchia. In the larger rock-cut tomb (Plate VII) the horizontal corona of the pediment is shown curved upwards at each end, resembling a reversed volute, the centre of which is carved with a head, and the cavetto cornice dies into the

[1] E. Douglas Van Buren in *Journal of Roman Studies*, IV (1914), 183.

[2] Giglioli in *Notizie degli Scavi*, 1919. 3.

[3] Van Buren in *Classical Review*, XX (1906) 77 *sqq.*

[4] A statement therefore such as that made by Fiechter (*Römische Mitteilungen*, XXI (1906), 254) that " the older podia are almost square or have a proportion of 5 : 6 of length to breadth ; with the increasing spread of the podium temple from Etruria over Latium and the South . . . the proportion gradually changes to 2 : 1 " is misleading.

top of this volute. The angle supports are piers which show either that the front of the temple of the third period (from which this tomb with its pedimental sculptures must undoutedly have been copied) sometimes consisted of four columns *in antis*—that is to say, the angle piers were the ends of the cella walls—or that for the sake of greater strength (requisite in the case of an Etruscan temple on account of the wide spacing of the columns) the angle supports consisted of square piers. In the tomb of the Tarquinii at Cervetri the square pier is surmounted by a strongly-developed cavetto capital, such as could only crown a square pier. This, however, is not the only type of capital found in the tombs ; there is a second variety, in which volutes form the chief decoration ; not the constructional volute of the Greek Ionic capital, but the decorative example such as is found in those from Cyprus. In the case of pilasters the lower part of the capital, below the cushion, is decorated at the angles with the anthemion ornament.

There is a second type of Ionic capital in the gateways at Perugia (Fig. 3, Plate V), which is probably a later development of the Greek Ionic volute. The dwarf pilasters which subdivide the decorative frieze above the gateway at Perugia have capitals in which a tendril supporting the anthemion rises between the volute and the egg and tongue moulding. In the capitals which crown the pilasters on each side of the arched opening above this frieze the egg and tongue is omitted, and a flower decorates the centre of the capital.

FIG. 4.

A further development of this capital, designed for a circular column, is found throughout Etruria, in which the volutes, still of Cyprian design, are more fully developed. Between them, on each face, is a head in full relief, and around the base of the capital a range of eight leaves (Fig. 4).